THE LIFE AND TIMES OF
A BOY IN KENTUCKY

Charleston, SC
www.PalmettoPublishing.com

The Life and Times of a Boy in Kentucky

First Edition

Hardcover ISBN: 979-8-8229-0280-0
Paperback ISBN: 979-8-8229-0281-7

ED ROULETTE

THE LIFE AND TIMES OF A BOY IN KENTUCKY

This is the story of my life from the earliest I can remember through my teenage years growing up in Northern Kentucky. It is not written in chronological order by age or times. It is written in snippets from my memories. It is the story of a boy of Kentucky.

I was born on March 1, 1943. Shortly after my birth, my father ran off with another woman. I was less than a year old, so I have no memory of this. My mother had to get a job to support my fifteen-year-old sister and my ten-year-old brother and me. My father did pay child support. Mother went to work at Monarchs Ice Cream Parlor in Covington, Kentucky. It was there she met my stepfather, who had gotten home from the army after World War II. It was around 1947 or 48. For at least the first couple years of my life, I was raised by my older sister and brother. I can still remember them listening to *Inner Sanctum*, a radio show, and being scared, so I would hide behind the couch. My early memories were of living above the railroad tracks in a rented house on a hill. I played in the yard with a couple of tin trucks and a few lead soldiers. Eventually my mother and stepfather got married, and we moved to a small house on the same road, but down from the railroad tracks. I shared a bed with my sister and brother. Around age twelve or thirteen, my brother moved in with our dad, as he was promised a horse. In court he chose Dad over Mom. He lived in the attic of my fraternal grandmother's log cabin. After that I saw less of him and missed him dearly.

My first bike I got for five dollars. It was my mother's friend's daughter's bike, so it was a girl's bike. I did not care. I rode it on the gravel roads, dirt roads, and grass. I rode it every day for hours within a couple hundred yards of home. Most of my friends were other young boys, and they all had boys' bikes, but they never cared that I was the only one riding a girl's bike. We were friends then and friends now. From the time I was around eleven, my friends and I would take a brown paper bag lunch and head to the hills surrounding our valley. We climbed trees, explored creeks, and had fantasy adventures as if we were cowboys or soldiers, pioneers or Indians.

I aways went to the little store and tavern down the road from my house from age around eleven or twelve and got bread or milk for my mom. The man who owned the store was a very nice old man. His wife had passed away several years before. One day I went there to cash in pop bottles I had picked up along the highway. It was early, so I was the only one in the store with him. I got two cents apiece for the ten bottles. That got me a soda and a Baby Ruth candy bar. As I sat and talked with him, he told me that he used to live in a house he still owned on the hill behind the store. He said it was about a couple hundred yards from the big creek that ran behind his store. He said the house wasn't much and he had moved into his store after the passing of his wife. He said he knew all of us young boys, and if we cleaned it up a little, we could use it as a clubhouse.

I was excited. My friends and I followed his directions to the old abandoned three-room houses. There were windows and a door opening, but no door. There was no glass in the windows. It was covered in dust inside and had tall grass around it in every direction. It was perfect. Soon there were six of us clearing brush and cutting weeds around the house. We borrowed brooms and swept the inside. It became our first and only clubhouse we ever had, and it was awesome. There was no road to the house, only a walking path. There was no well or water. It was a shell of what it had once been, but to young boys it was paradise. Over a few weeks we came up with old straight-backed chairs and an old couch that was headed to the dump. In our eyes it just couldn't have gotten any better. Now we formed a loose, nit club or gang and had our second home away from home. As the years went by, our little club dissolved, but a few of us went there from time to time through our teen years.

About my mom. She was born in Lexington, Kentucky. She had an older sister and two brothers. She was married at sixteen and had my older sister when she was seventeen. Her sister was married and lived in Cincinnati, Ohio. Her brothers owned a company that did drywall, plastering, and painting. Mom was a great southern cook and was also the boss. She made almost every decision about our lives, including my stepfather's.

My older brother dropped out of school in the tenth grade and got a job working on cars. He became a great transmission repairman years later and provided well for his family. My older sister was married, and her husband, Al, was a junior. He was in Korea in 1952 in the army fighting in the Korean war. Until her passing, Mom was the glue that held our family together.

About my stepfather. He was abandoned by his mother and left on the porch of her parents in Jonesville, Kentucky. His grandparents did not really want him but had little choice. He had to drop out of school in the third grade to work on their farm. Little is known about his life with them, and as soon as he could, he joined the army and spent most of World War II in France and Germany. He never learned how to read and write. He therefore held many different jobs like digging ditches, maintenance, janitor, and handyman, and he worked in the hayfields or helped with tobacco. He was a good man and a wonderful stepfather. He refused to spank any of his stepchildren. That he left up to Mom. She administered all punishment from spanking to time in your room. He and my mother rest together in eternal peace in Kentucky. She passed first in 1988, and he in 1992.

About my brother. Jim was six feet, five inches tall. He was energetic and played hardball and softball on different teams. He was an avid hunter, primarily rabbits and squirrels. He married a local girl, and they had three daughters. They had hoped one would be a boy, but it was not to be. My brother was a great shot and won a championship shooting trap in a national competition in Vandalia, Ohio. He always lived in Northern Kentucky. My brother was very good to me, and when we were young, he taught me how to hunt and about gun safety. My first gun was a single-shot .22, and I could hunt only with my real dad or my brother. At age eleven I guess they discussed it, and for the first time, with my .22 and three shells, I was allowed to go alone in my grandmother's woods. I found a hickory nut tree where the nutshell droppings meant squirrels were eating there. About an hour before dark, a gray squirrel came into the tree, and I shot him. My first of many solo hunts for squirrels and rabbits. They were not killed for fun but for a source of meat for my grandmother. My brother passed away at age forty-four in 1979. He died from cancer that started in his appendix. My son was born in 1964, and I named him after my brother, who spent some time knowing him. The loss of my brother was a devastating loss, as was my mother's years later.

Later in my youth, I mentioned going into the USAF and wanting to be stationed in California or on the West Coast. My brother asked me why. I told him I wanted to see new things, have new adventures, and see the Pacific Ocean. I will never forget his reply. He said, "If you want to travel, we can go see the Smoky Mountains, and as for as wanting to see water, jump in my truck, and we can go sit by the Ohio River." My brother never failed to be my mentor and friend. He always had a great sense of humor and humility. He repaired a lot of people's cars for little or no money even after working hard at a regular auto mechanic's job. I will always miss him, and I think of him every day. He will always, like Mom, live in my memory forever.

About Grandma, my dad's mother. She was my only living grandparent. My grandfather died when I was five, and I remember only that he had a dog named Cappy. So for my life, there was only Grandma. I stayed at her house at least three or four weekends a month. It was my base for my trips to hunt in the surrounding hills and woods. I slept in the attic in a featherbed winter, summer, spring, or fall. Grandma knew many interesting stories.

She had a cow and a hog and raised chickens and later turkeys. She was as energetic as any young person. She had an old barn that was in bad repair and a saltwater and a freshwater well. The path to the freshwater well was lined by every color hollyhock flower you could imagine. I would take two two-gallon buckets to the freshwater well, crank the handle, and bring back the water for her. The path there and back was lined with flowers taller than me.

Once since I thought I was a pioneer, a friend and I started building a log cabin on top of the hill above Grandma's farm, which was about a hundred acres or so. After chopping down several trees, notching them, and stacking them, we quit at about three logs high. It was too much work for young boys. I found Grandpa's dairy, and it had a map of an Indian mound he had found on top of the hill. He had recovered a few items, but he thought there were more. A friend and I took shovels and excavated the spot until we were exhausted. The result: we found nothing. Dreams of discovery do not always end with a discovery, but sometimes with disappointment.

Grandma attended church every Sunday. Sometimes she walked, but as she got older, she got a ride to and from. She lived to be ninety-eight or ninety-nine years old, the last year and a half in a nursing home. She had dementia, and her mind wandered in and out. I went to visit her, and some days she remembered who I was, and some she had no clue. Her name was Eva, and one day my dad asked her, "Do you know who I am?" She replied, "Of course I do—you are my father." My dad said he knew he looked old, but hardly that old.

Grandmas are a gift given to us, if we are lucky, and bring joy and wisdom to our lives. Eva may be gone, but she will never be forgotten. She made butter and whipped cream fresh from the cow. She made me gingerbread and homemade bread. Now whenever I eat gingerbread, I put whipped cream on it, and I know Grandma is smiling down. Like my mother, I loved my grandmother.

Our rented house was small; we had an outhouse and no indoor plumbing. We got our water from a well and heated it on a wooden stove. We took turns bathing in a big round washtub. Bath time for us was an ordeal. For my twelfth birthday, my stepfather rode a bus to Covington and came back home with my present: a twenty-six-inch green-and-white boy's bike. I felt like a king. I was named after my mother's brother while he was in the Seabees during World War II. He smoked black IBold cigars, loved Buicks, and had a nice boat. He came over every Sunday, and the grown men played horseshoes, and we had homemade ice cream.

Sometime in 1952 my real father went to a local feed store to pick up feed for Grandma's chickens. He knew I loved watching the ducks fly in and swim in a local pond. He showed up and brought me a baby duck. I could keep it at Grandma's or, if Mom approved, where I lived. After I begged and pleaded, Mom gave in, and so began the story of a duck named Junior.

The saga of Junior Duck. When I got the duck, I thought he was a male. I kept him in a cardboard box in the kitchen. He had a bowl of water to drink or play in and cracked corn, oats, rice, and seeds to eat. Unlike children, ducks age fast. His yellow feathers soon became white, and he was outgrowing his box. So to keep him safe from predators, he was kept in a storge shed on straw for a bed, and I would let him out and stay by his side. We had a small creek that was by our house, so he and I would head to the creek. Soon he was eating aquatic plants, minnows, and bugs along with shelled corn. When Junior was about seven months old, it snowed, and by then he was running up and down the creek having a blast. He was well insulated from the cold. By the little creek was a patch of yellow jonquils. They looked beautiful against the white snow, and Junior was sitting right in the middle of the patch. When he saw me, he squawked, quacked, and came running. We were pals. Now came a big, big surprise: where Jr. was setting were six large duck eggs. Jr. my male duck was really Jr. my female hen duck. I was shocked but happy as I gathered the eggs and took them to show my mother. Everyone in my family had assumed Junior was a male. I refused to change *my* duck's name. So the duck remained named Junior.

One day I came home from school, and I noticed Junior was limping. She had received a leg injury. Within minutes a neighbor came by and said Junior had pecked his dog in the eye, and it was blinded in one eye. Fortunately, another neighbor lad saw the whole incident. The small dog had chased the duck, who'd tried to escape, but the dog had caught her by the leg, and the duck defended herself in the only way she could. The duck was in our yard; the dog was uninvited and trespassing, so the matter was closed.

After that, if the dog saw Junior out and about, he ran home fast. Junior would walk with a limp the rest of her life with a leg that remained swollen. She wobbled like she had been at a moonshine still, and yes, there were some around. Junior was more like a dog than a duck. She followed me around the neighborhood. When the seventeen-year locusts emerged, Junior gorged herself until she could not walk. Lying there, if a locust got in range, she would extend her long neck and gobble it down. Fearing she would eat herself to death, I put her once again in the shed for a short while until the locusts were gone.

When I was about fifteen, I got off the bus and walked the gravel road home. I knew something was wrong, for Junior always came to see me when I came into the yard. I went looking for her and found her lifeless body lying in the creek she loved. I had lost a friend. She had led a good duck's life for nearly eleven years. When I told my mother, she cried. I got a shovel from the shed, dug a deep hole, wrapped Junior Duck in an old towel, and buried her by the creek she loved. It was hard to lose a pet who had become a friend to this boy: Junior the Duck.

When winter comes and the lakes are half-frozen over, I sometimes go watch the wild mallard ducks fly in to eat and rest on their way south. I take corn to feed them, as bread is not good for them. I found if I sit on the bank and throw corn out on the bank a few feet in front of me, they will slowly gain the nerve and come and eat it, all the while keeping an eye on me. In time and with patience, I can even eventually hand-feed some of the bolder wild ducks. This makes me happy and yet sad. I wish Junior had had the chance to fly with the flock. Perhaps she did in her dreams.

The swimming hole. There was a swimming hole in the creek near our house. It was about a half mile away. The water was about four to five feet deep, and it measured about sixty feet across and ninety feet long. There was a small tree with a forked branch, and we would take turns jumping into the water. On a hot summer day there were usually about seven or eight boys there playing in the water. We were all nine to twelve years of age and had a blast. It was cooling and fun. The water was deep enough to swim but also easy to stand up and keep your head above water.

Summer fun came to a halt when polio came along. No one knew the cause. A boy from our area came down with the disease, and parents were scared—very scared. The boy had been swimming in the same creek at another pool of water. It was getting hotter by the day in Kentucky, and the water was flowing slowly, and there was stagnation at the end of our swimming hole. Word quickly spread that perhaps the stagnant water was the cause. My mother sat me down and told me the creek was off limits. No wading and no swimming. Being a typical boy, I listened but sneaked off to the woods above our house and walked down the railroad tracks and down to the swimming hole. It was hot; the water was cool. Immediately I noticed there were only a couple other friends there. We were the slick ones. We had all been told not to go to the creek but did anyway. After an hour or so, I reversed path and came back home. My mother ask me where I had been. I *lied* and said in the woods. She knew I was lying, as my hair was still wet. First I got scolded and then spanked. Once again, she laid down the law about *no creek*!

After a day or two, I figured what she did not know would not hurt. So once again I *lied*. I told her I was going to walk up the road and play marbles with a few other guys. She said OK. So I did walk up the road; however, once out of sight, I again cut through a field and back to the creek. This time I felt I was good. I had sneaked an old hand towel out of the house hidden in my shirt. I swam in the creek for a couple of hours. Dried my hair well. Waited about an hour and came home. My mom asked me, "How did your marble game go?" "It went well," I *lied*. She knew I was lying again. She could smell the creek in my hair. Once again a lecture, a deserved spanking, and grounded for a whole week to the house and chores. When you are a boy, you think you are smart, clever, and invincible. Sometimes the ego takes you down the forbidden path. I found out mothers are the gatekeepers of the right path. Being hardheaded or slow to learn got me spankings and groundings, lessons I would take into adulthood. As far as I know, the creek was not the cause of polio, but I will never be sure.

I played trumpet in the band in high school. I got a superior rating on my trumpet solo at state, on a brass quartet, and a trumpet trio. Our band also got a superior rating. Our band director was a wonderful musician. Sadly, he lost his life in the Beverly Hills Country Club fire while entertaining with an orchestra. I thought I wanted to be a professional trumpet player. My band director played woodwinds, so he arranged for me to go take lessons from the lead trumpet player of the Cincinnati Orchestra. I did. To be great, I was told to practice six hours a day every day. I did for a few months but realized I was missing out on other things. I sold my trumpet before I enlisted in the USAF.

In high school when I was a sophomore, four of us started a German band for fun. I played trumpet. We had a sax player, a trombone player, and a clarinet player. We added a tuba player and named our German band Um Pa Pa. We got asked to play in two different churches. We played in a teen cantina. It was more jokes than music. We hammed it up and got lots of laughs. We got invited to play for an Eastern Star meeting, as one of the boy's aunts was the grand matron. They had not told us, and we did not know they were going to end with what they called a grand march. They ask if we could play any marching music. We knew none. As we pondered what we could do to let them march, our sax player said, "Why not play our school song?" We did. It was played at football games. The words, if sung, begin with, "Here come the Pioneers." It worked, and everyone was happy. We played for fun and not money. Once a church wanted to give us twenty-five dollars. We told them no, but in a good gesture they donated it to the band fund. Um Pa Pa lasted about a year, and then we all had too many irons in the fire with school, jobs, and girls.

The magical decade. The 1950s: days of sock hops. Roller rinks, school dances, teen canteens. Hayrides, double dates, and fun. The cars were awesome, and cruising the town was a Friday- or Saturday-night event. No one can ever forget the Studebakers, Chevrolets, Fords, Oldsmobiles, Hudsons, Nashes, Pontiacs, Buicks, and other cars from the grandest era of the automobile. Times were slower, schools educated, families were closer, and life was good for most. Even though my family was on the poorer side, we hardly noticed, as we had a great garden. My mother and older sister would can vegetables for winter, and we always had chickens and eggs. What we lacked in money, we made up in love of family. The 50s are when I grew from child to boy to man. My friends and I pooled our money and put gas in someone's car and headed to the drag strip. We watched the races, drank Cokes, ate hot dogs, and enjoyed life.

A history of work. My very first paid job was cutting kindling for an elderly lady. My Grandmother told me Calleta needed a boy to cut and stack wood for her to start a fire in her Warm Morning stove. I got the job. I would split some small logs for her and stack them in a bin inside her small house. She paid me a dime, and I was thrilled. She was nice, friendly, and gracious, and I would usually stay for a cup of tea and talk with her for a little while. My next paid job was a little harder. I worked in the hayfields of a local farmer. I struggled to set hay bales on the back of a wagon while his wife drove the tractor. He stacked them high. The bales weighed almost as much as I did, it seemed, and I would start lifting them with both hands and my knee. We would work an hour and take a ten-minute break. We usually worked five or six hours in the hot sun and were done. I got ten cents a bale for helping and was treated nicely.

When I turned sixteen, I got a driver's license. I did not yet have a car to drive. I had one, but it was not roadworthy. A man lived in the neighborhood, and he built rock driveway walls and rock houses. He needed help, as his worker had died. I went to his house to ask for a job. I was skinny and weighed about 140 pounds. He explained he was looking for a man, and I did not fit the bill. His wife was friends at church with my mother, so she told him he should at least give me a chance. To appease her, he did. He had a one-ton dump truck, and he took me to the creek. There was a granite rock ledge, and he had his wife follow us to give him a ride. He said, "Here is a sledgehammer and a pick." He told me to break pieces off the rock ledge and load the truck. He found out I had a license, and he lived about a mile away. He worked for the railroad and asked if I knew how to drive a stick shift. I said I could. He left, and I started busting rocks and throwing them into the bed of the truck. In five hours, I had a large load, and so I came back to his house. I did not know where he wanted the rocks dumped or how to operate the dump. He came out, looked at the load, and asked, after he left, how many of my friends helped me. I said none. He said, "I am going to pay you a day's pay, ten dollars for the load. Now, how many friends helped you? And do not lie." He was a grown man, and I was a boy. I said, "I told you the truth; you have thought I lied. I did not. If you go back to the creek with me, I will load your truck again." He reached in his pocket, handed me a ten-dollar bill, and said, "I will see you tomorrow about eight a.m." I got the job.

Over the next couple of years, I mixed mortar, loaded rocks, dug foundations for driveway walls, and got stronger. I got paid ten dollars a day if we worked two hours or ten hours. He bought our lunch every day, and we always took an hour. It was a great job, and he was a great man to work with. I learned a lot about work, work ethic, and life.

I loved playing basketball in the neighborhood, and so when I was a senior, I tried out for the high school basketball team. I made it but was not put on the varsity, but on the JV team. I played and had fun. We won some and lost some. It came time for the last game of the season. The varsity coach told me I would dress varsity for that game and may even get to start. I guess that was a goodwill gesture. The school had ordered me a jacket, which was to be presented at the game, I suppose. I thought it over and told the coach I *quit*. I felt if I was not good enough to have made the varsity, I was not good enough to be displayed as a show dog. So, during the last game, I sat in the stands with the pep band. I have never regretted that decision one bit. I cheered for both the JV and varsity games, as I had done ninth through eleventh grade. Right or wrong, I stand on the principle, which suits me.

In grade school and high school, I met a lot of boys and girls. I am still friends with many of them today. The sad thing about life is as the years pass and memories fade, you lose contact. If you were ever my friend, you still are. These were the good old days of my life. Some things were not that good, like outdoor toilets and no running water in the house. What makes them good is that family and friends were young, vibrant, and alive. Doors were left unlocked, and neighborhoods were safe. The good old days were the *good old days* indeed.

The overnight campout. One day while exploring the hills a few miles from my house, I stumbled across an old cemetery. It was in a clearing between a group of large pines surrounding it. It did have some overgrowth, but the tombstones were quite visible. As I read the stones, I noticed they were all dated from the late 1800s to the early 1900s. What a discovery. I told my mother and stepfather about the place. I also told every boy in the neighborhood. It was a great find, and a day or so later, five of us set out early with our sack lunches and once again came to the cemetery. After we looked around, we sat down in the grass and laughed and joked. We talked of vampires, werewolves, goblins, ghosts, and every other imaginable creature of the night. This is what boys do. Bravery in the light of day. We were all ten to thirteen, the thirteen-year-old being the oldest and boldest. So out of nowhere, he came up with an idea. We should all spend the night in this old cemetery. It was a dare.

Not wanting to appear to be a scaredy-cat, we all said it was a great idea. Once again, false bravado. So we made a pact and told our parents we were camping out in the field at one of our friend's houses. They had a small farm. The next afternoon we all met around six o'clock after the evening meal. With full bellies and a couple of canteens, we set out for our secret location. All five us showed up, and we first topped at a nearby tavern / general store and bought a dollar's worth of penny candy for the trip. We stuck to the farm campout story, as there were a few adults there. I never will forget the old man who ran the place saying, "You boys have fun!"

We arrived at our destination in good spirits and prepared to prove we were the bravest of the brave. Everything was fine. Outside the area of the tombstones, we built a small fire. Two of our boys were Boy Scouts, and they had brought matches and did a good job. We sat ins a semicircle around the fire and ate penny candy, sharing the canteens of water. We were having a good time. Around 9:30 p.m. it was dark, but we had decided in our pact to stay up all night, so we sat and lay on the ground. In summer it did not get cold at night, so we were roughing it. Sometime, I guess around midnight, the fire was burning low. One boy had a flashlight, so we decided to let the fire burn out. Off in the distance, a dog or coyote howled. That was when the rubber hit the road. Someone said that the howl sounded like the werewolf in the movie he saw at the drive-in with his family. It was the film with Lon Chaney. After the third howl, someone said, "I want to get out of here!" Now imagination took over. Another voice: "If you go, I am too." Soon it was unanimous. In the dark of night, we all ran down the hill toward my yard. Of course, we received a few cuts from blackberry bushes, a few scrapes, and a couple bruises, but no serious injury. In the morning when my stepfather came outside, there were five boys sleeping on the ground. Many years later and after retiring from the USAF, I walked the hills again. I never could find that old cemetery, and if I did, the thought of spending a night there never crossed my mind.

Winter in Kentucky. Cold and snow: what every boy and girl wanted in winter. Sleds and sledding were big in our neighborhood. We had hills all around. As soon as we got home from school, off came the school clothes and on went the playclothes. I grabbed my sled and headed to the big hill above the pasture near my house. Soon the hill would be packed with ten or fifteen sleds. I would sled ride until it got too dark to see and would be freezing cold when I got home. I would get out of all my wet clothes, dry off, and put on warm clothes. We had a Warm Morning stove, and I would sit close to it and warm up. Mom would make hot chocolate, and my sister would pop popcorn. On the weekends we would build snow forts and have snowball fights or build snowmen. Winter was also the time as I got older that I went rabbit hunting. I tried my hand at trapping muskrats but only got a few.

The greatest event in winter was Christmas. In the life of any child from 1 to 101, it is a time of joy and giving. It was my mother's favorite holiday. It still is mine. I love seeing the lights, ornaments, and decorations on a Christmas tree. Most importantly it is a time to celebrate the birth of our savior. To some, winter may be bleak, overcast, and miserable, but it is to me a season of joy and happiness. Lucky is the man or woman who lives where there are four distinct seasons. Each brings a promise of what is good if looked for.

The cherry tree. In my grandmother's side yard was a cherry tree. Every year it produced beautiful and tasty red cherries. During a bad storm, the cherry tree was hit by lightning and split almost in half. Grandma was disappointed. The tree had been planted by her log cabin when she was first married. As a boy I would get a ladder and a bucket and pick the ripe cherries. They made wonderful cherry pie, cherry cobbler, and cherry jelly. My grandmother loved the tree. It had been good to her, bringing forth a bounty of cherries for many seasons. Even in bloom, cherry trees are amazing with their beauty. After the lightning strike, my real father, who lived in a house next door, came and looked at the tree. One side of it was dead and looked it. What to do? His first thought was to saw it down; Grandma said no, give it time. I agreed with Grandma. Time passed. When the cherry blossoms bloomed again, they bloomed only on the good side of the tree. When the cherries came in, once again I filled buckets with cherries. When all the cherries were harvested, my grandmother and father were amazed. The half tree had produced practically the same amount!

The elm tree and the freshwater well. In 1949 I was still five years old when Mom called me into the house and told me my grandpa had passed away. I barely knew my grandpa. I remember he had a dog named Cappy, and he sat in the side yard and chewed Red Man tobacco. Everything else I ever knew about him came from my real dad or my grandmother. At five I did not fully understand death and dying. As I grew, I found out Grandpa had been a violin teacher, a gambler, and a small man. When he married Grandma, they bought one hundred acres with a log cabin. It was a farm. From what I have gathered, Grandma was a much better farmer than Grandpa. He suffered from illness a lot and spent the last few years of his life mostly bedridden.

After Grandpa died, things started to happen. When I was ten or eleven, Dad told me the elm tree must have gotten some kind of disease, and it was dying. I had a bow and arrow. Dad tied a string to an arrow, and I shot it over the top of the elm tree. Dad tied a rope to the string and pulled it over a large dead branch. I got way out of the way, and with a tractor, he was able to bring the dead limb down. We repeated this string roping of several dead branches and took down four or five. A bad windstorm could have broken any of them off and hit Grandma's roof. Problem averted, but the elm kept on dying. Finally, Dad got a neighbor of his who came with a chainsaw and cut the tree down so it fell in the pasture and not on the house. The elm tree was gone; only the stump remained.

When I was twelve, the freshwater well went dry. It had been spring fed for many years, but no more. Dad brought Grandma water from his house every day until he had a large tank built or bought, and a water truck delivered water. To the day he died, my dad always said the farm had died with Grandpa. I have never thought the farm died but was kept alive by Grandma as best she could.

My Grandmother always had a cow. She had a couple Jerseys, one at a time, and a Guernsey. If remember right, she had three different milk cows over many years. She named them all the same name. Why I will never know, but she named them Daisy. I guess she liked the name. I found that odd. She also had a sow pig and she named it Susie. Pictures of Grandma when she was sixteen show her as a beautiful young girl. Grandma was four feet, ten inches tall. As she aged, she still had a radiant glow about her and a great smile. She had a beautiful lilac bush that smelled wonderful, and she would cut flowers from it for the people she went to church with. I never heard one person speak anything but good about my grandma: my hero.

The New Hampshire reds and rats in the rosebush. When we moved into a better rented house, it had a chicken coup and a chicken wire fence. No chickens. After saving a few dollars in hayfield money, I bought six baby chicks. My stepfather had raised chickens, so he helped me to get them started. Within a year we had egg layers and a rooster. Now we were in the chicken business of gathering eggs and having fried chicken. I knew little about chickens when we began, and when I asked for Rhode Island reds, the man at the feed store told me he only had New Hampshire reds. Since I did not know the difference and did not care, I said OK. Raising chickens is easy. You give them feed, and they peck around and eat anything on the ground they find.

Our chicken pen was large and the henhouse well built. That was done by the owners, who lived in a new house just down the gravel road. Once we lost a chicken or two to a weasel. My stepfather and I moved the chickens to a storage shed and left two chickens in the pen. The second night, the weasel came calling. The weasel was shot with a .12-gauge. No more Mr. Weasel ever. Everything was back to normal. We were kept in eggs and chicken to eat.

My uncle came over on Sunday, and after dinner, he was sitting facing a fencerow that bordered the yard. He saw something move in the rosebush, which covered about fifty feet of fence. After looking closely, he told my stepfather and me to come look. In the rosebush were several rats. I had never seen them before, and my uncle hadn't either. Evidently the rats had taken up home living in the rosebush. Now my mother and sister would not go near the bush. So, a trip to the store, and DECON doomed the rats, and the problem went away. Once again, my mother and sister could go pick the bright-red roses without worry.

Making money. One day while roaming the hills, a friend and I found a large blackberry patch. We ate a few and ran home and got buckets. We picked two five-gallon buckets full of blackberries. There were many more, and we even found another patch close by. No one know who owned the property, and there were no residences even close. No cows or anything to indicate it was being used for anything. My friend and I kept the location a secret and picked blackberries. After our moms had enough, we went up and down Old 17 Road and sold blackberries door to door. We ended up with five dollars, and when you are a boy in the 50s, you feel rich. We helped the economy by buying penny candy, candy cigarettes, candy bars, soda, chips, and moon pies. That was our first joint venture.

We found out we could buy watermelons from a farmer for twenty-five cents. So, we pooled our money and bought four. We loaded them in a little red wagon and went to every house on the road. We sold them for fifty cents. We went back and got eight more and again went door to door in the subdivision up the street. Finally, a woman bought the last two. We were worn out. Back to the store. This time we each kept a quarter. The rest was invested in, you guessed it, candy, soda, chips, and moon pies.

My entire life when I was young, I lived near the L&N railroad tracks. I saw steam locomotives and the diesels. The noise never bothered me, and I even liked the horns when the trains came to crossings. I always stood about fifty feet at least from the trains, and usually the engineers would wave. I was playing ball in a field using rocks for bases with several other boys. We all had a glove, and there were two bats and one ball. The hardball we had was rubber coated and had been well used. Our little make-up field was below the train tracks. There was a black cinder hill from the train tracks down to the edge of our little field. Quite often someone would hit one up almost to the tracks on the top of the hill.

Once when we were playing, a railroad crew with two grown men came to work on a crossing, and they were in a handcar. Someone hit the ball, and it landed about ten feet up the cinder hill and about fifty feet from them. One of the men grabbed the ball, and we thought he was going to throw it down to us. He did not. Now you had a bunch of boys yelling, "Throw our ball back—it's the only one we have." The men ignored us. There were ten of us in the little field. So we got up our nerve, went farther down, and climbed up on the railroad. Now we were within forty or fifty feet of the two grown men and once again nicely asked for our ball back. One of the men told us where we could go and said we were trespassing on railroad property.

What to do? The railroad had stones just the perfect size for throwing. So we spread out on both sides of the tracks, grabbed handfuls of rocks, and said, "If you do not give us the ball, we will throw rocks at you and the handcar." Both men got angry and yelled a few obscenities, and one threw the ball down the gravel road we all lived on. We got back down, got the ball, and watched them leave. We thought it was over. Soon a pickup truck pulled up, and a man from the railroad got out and said we had been playing on the tracks and had thrown rocks at his workers and their handcar. The grown men had lied. We told the man the truth, and fortunately the man, who lived in a house across the gravel road, knew us and knew we played ball there every day.

That is when I learned about compromise. We agreed to move home plate back about two hundred feet and stay off the railroad's property. We did move home plate back as promised and the bases. We would never hit the ball on the cinder hill again. It was out of our hitting distance. We had to work on our makeshift ball field and smooth out the ground. Eventually we got a new baseball, and the game continued. At that point in my life, I decided since those men had lied, I would walk the railroad tracks whenever I wanted. And I did.

When I was sixteen, our church sponsored a Boy Scout troop. They made the decision to start an Explorer Post. I was the president of a Sunday school youth group, so we talked about it, and seven of us older teenage boys joined. It was fun, and we go to go to a big powwow camping event called Peter Loon. We learned how to tie several different knots, basic first aid, and how to start a fire. One summer our scout leader took us on a local farm with permission for a campout overnight. We sat up our tents and that night sat around the campfire and toasted marshmallows. One of the boys went beyond the light of the fire and came back and said there were glowing eyes watching. We laughed until we followed him and saw what looked like a whole bunch of glowing eyes. Our scout leader saw them and shined a flashlight in their direction, and they disappeared. He turned the light off, and they were back again. To say the least, it was a little creepy seeing such an eerie glow. Finally, we all went to sleep, and the next day we packed our gear and walked out of the woods to the leader's pickup truck to head home. We stopped and thanked the property owner and told him what we saw and thought maybe they were some kind of animal. He got a big laugh out of that and explained to us it was foxfire generated by decaying wood. We all learned.

We had a couple fundraisers and built up a little over $100 in our treasury. We also paid token dues of a dime or some small amount each week to support the troop's functions. We had a meeting scheduled for a Wednesday evening to plan an event. We were there, but the scoutmaster did not show up. Soon we found out that he had left his rented house a mess, had not paid rent for a couple months, and had skipped to parts unknown. Two of us had a meeting with our deacons, elders, and pastor and quit the scouts. We were not mad. We felt sorry that the scoutmaster had not had the decency to swallow his pride and reveal his problems to us and the church. Our pastor prayed he might find peace and prosperity. That has aways been good enough for me. Our Sunday school youth group still had many fun events. We went sled riding together twice a month. We went to the greenhouse in Eden Park in Cincinnati and to the Garden of Hope in Covington, Kentucky, where there was a replica of the tomb Jesus was laid in. We put on pageants at Easter and Christmas with all the church children. It was good times.

When I was about six years old, I got a rabbit for Easter. He was a pet and not for eating. I had him in a rabbit cage and would take him out and let him eat grass in our side yard. I fed him rabbit pellets as his normal food and mad sure he had plenty of water. I named him Bugs Bunny like the cartoon rabbit. He never tried to run away and was easy to catch, as he would come to be petted like a dog, and I would put him back in his cage, where he was safe. In a nearby field was a green apple tree, and all us boys and girls would go there and eat an apple or two. They were sour but good. One day I gave one to Bugs, and he loved it. Being a kid and not knowing much about rabbits, I went to the apple tree and filled a sack with the green apples. I put them all in his cage so he could eat them when he wanted. The next morning my stepfather saw Bugs lying in his cage. He was dead. I was sad. Trying to be good to my bunny, I had made the mistake that cost him his life. He was the first pet I lost. I buried him under a sycamore tree on a bank overlooking the creek. I cried.

Growing up, I always had a dog. My first dog was a big mixed-breed cur. His name was Spot. He was one tough dog. He went with me everywhere. He would walk beside me down the gravel road as I waited for the school bus. After I was on the bus looking out the window, I would see him running back home. When I got off the bus, he would be there waiting for me and walk home with me. Dogs must have a built-in clock, as this behavior is well documented. One day I was playing in the creek near a rock ledge, and suddenly Spot growled and went after a snake that was close to me. It was a copperhead, and he killed it. He also yelped in pain and ran off. He had been bitten. My friends, my stepfather, and my older brother searched the creek and even the hills close by. There was no sign of my dog. A week passed, and then a farmer stopped by and asked my stepfather if we were missing a black-and-white-spotted dog. Yes, we were. I was in school. Spot had made it to the farmer's cow pond and was lying there for days with his legs in the mud. My stepfather brought him home, and for the first time he was allowed in the house and lay on a blanket. He had not eaten for several days, and my mother fixed him soup and gave him a leftover pork chop. He got better every day and within a week was up and about. He had been saved by the mud in the pond, which must have drawn most of the poison out, was all we could figure. That was the first time I had ever seen a copperhead but certainly not the last.

Almost all young boys would go to the creek and catch banded water snakes. They were nonvenomous, and I never knew anyone who was bit playing with them. It was common for goys to come by and show me a banded water snake or black snake they had caught. Most parents would not let them keep the snake, so they were set free and went back to whatever it is snakes do. One day a neighbor boy came by, and I was standing on the little footbridge that crossed our creek. He was about six years old and had a snake. I looked at the snake and yelled for my stepfather to come look at it. He was holding it in the middle, and its head and tail were hanging down. My stepfather told him to drop it in the creek. He did not want to and said, "I want to keep it." My stepfather told him if he would drop it in the creek, he would give him a quarter. He dropped the snake in the creek. My stepfather gave him a quarter, and he took off for the store to buy as much candy as he could. My stepfather got a shovel and cut the snake's head off. It was a copperhead.

This is how this came about. There was an old Model A Ford that sat in a field near us for as long as I could remember. The boy had spotted the snake, which was headed down a hole. Its tail was sticking out as it was slithering down. He grabbed its tail. The snake was headfirst in the hole and kept trying to pull away. The boy held on. The snake could not turn around, so it kept trying to go down the hole. The boy continued to hold on. After who knows how long, the boy pulled the snake out of the hole and was taking him home. What probably saved the boy was the snake was worn out from the struggle. My stepfather made it a point to go to the boy's house and got the story of how this had happened. The boy's dad was grateful. The boy had been told not to play with snakes. I believe he got his little behind spanked. I knew that boy for many years, and I never saw him with a snake. I believe he had learned his lesson. He was lucky.

One Christmas I got a record player and a 45 record. One was Buddy Holly, and the record was *Peggy Sue*. I had a first cousin, and I thought the song was written about her. No one told me different, so I thought that for a long time. Her older sister was a gifted singer and performed at local shows. I saw very little of them growing up, as they lived in Ohio, which seemed a long way from us. We did not have a car, so I guess a distance of about fifteen miles is a long way. The few times we went to their house, they would go get the kaleidoscope, and I would be fascinated looking in it at the colors and changing patterns. The most fascinating thing about their house was they had running water, electric lights, and an indoor bathroom. In my mind they were rich; in reality they were middle class.

When I was a boy, you could still find arrowheads once in a while. It happened sometimes when people were plowing a new spot for a garden. The log cabin my grandmother lived in had supposedly withstood an attack by the Shawnee Indians. Grandma had pictures of the cabin before they moved in, and it did still have a small hole to fit in below the staircase. She said it also had few windows and did have gun slits. I do know when she plowed a garden with a handheld push plow, she found three unique arrowheads, which she kept for me. Once my grandfather found a stone axe stuck in a tree. That was before I was born. I heard the story but never saw it. I did see, however, one knife and one sword from the Civil War. The story passed down was that they had been found in a field after a battle in which several men had been killed. I do not know which side the weapons were from. I only know what I was told, and I did see them.

Grandma had a display cabinet, and in it were eight of the prettiest glasses I had ever seen. Four of them were bloodred with a gold ring around the top. Four of them were bloodred but had white flowers etched on them. I liked them so much Grandma was going to give them to me when I was around sixteen or seventeen. I would not take them, for Grandma was getting older, and I knew how much she loved them and the many quilts she had made. I felt that Grandma lived because of her religion and generosity. She raised and gave away lots of flowers many times to people at her church. She very seldom sold a quilt from a big trunk but did give them away. Years later Grandma made me a quilt, which I kept at Mom's house for the first few years I was in the USAF. Grandma knew I was going, so the quilt was red, white, and blue. I had it for over twenty years.

I closed one chapter of my life and began a twenty-plus-year chapter of the second stage. From as early as I can remember until I left home, Mom always made a spice cake with caramel icing for my birthday. She also made my favorite meal, navy bean soup with ham and cornbread. We ate together as a family every day. One of our favorite desserts was homemade strawberry shortcake with lots of whipped cream. It seems no matter the financial situation, we ate well. Family money was sometimes scarce, but we always had plenty of homegrown or home-raised food. I remember being hungry in the evenings, and we always had popcorn with butter. Life was good.

The first time I ever saw a television was at our landlord's house. TV was just becoming available, and there were only a few programs aired. It was only on a few hours a day. The first thing we saw was an old Tom Mix western. It was amazing. We were all amazed. One early evening we got invited over to see wrestling. That was the first time I had ever seen such a thing, and the wrestling hero was named Don Eagle. We finally got our own black-and-white TV when I was sixteen. The picture was fuzzy, and the indoor antenna worked poorly, but we had TV. We were proud. TV was coming into its own. There was more programming and more shows available. TV went off the air around midnight, and the last thing was the playing of "The Star-Spangled Banner."

I always knew from my junior year in high school I was going to join the military. I had not decided on which branch. I did not tell my family or my friends. But I knew. My uncle had been in the navy Seabees and my stepfather in the army. Neither talked of their service, and both had seen action in World War II. I admired them both, but that admiration had nothing to do with my decision. In 1962, Vietnam was getting revved up, so after I graduated, I worked for Decca Records in their warehouse as a stock boy for a short while. I told no one but stopped by the recruiting office in Covington. I listened carefully to the options I was offered. So I liked the air force option best. I also liked the fact that the uniform looked good to me. I tested in Fort Thomas and passed the test. My highest score was in admin. Second was mechanic. And last was electronics. My brother was a mechanic. So that was what I chose. Then I would be given a choice of what kind of mechanic. So I chose jet engines, as I had always liked airplanes. I kept this to myself still. I took the physical and passed. There was an opening that I could fill in the next week. I took it. I went home and called my brother and older sister and ask if they could come to Mom's; I wanted to talk to them. That was when I told my family. That was one of the few times I saw my mother cry. After the shock wore off, she understood it was a chance for a boy from

Kentucky to do something he really wanted to do. July 9, 1962, was the day I took my first airplane ride. Many would follow out of the airport in Northern Kentucky to San Antonio. It is what I considered to be the end of my journey from boy to man.

Lightning Source UK Ltd.
Milton Keynes UK
UKHW020154091122
411883UK00020B/116/J